About the Author: Gerri Moore

Gerri Moore is a mother, Registered Nurse, coach, mentor, trainer and resilient storyteller who lives in Leicester, UK. With a professional background in personal development, emotional intelligence, and neuro-linguistic programming (NLP), Gerri combines her lived experiences with her deep understanding of human behaviour to inspire and support others through life's most challenging moments.

Her debut memoir, *Lauren's Story – A Lost Future*, was born from the raw heartbreak of losing her nine-week-old daughter Lauren to Sudden Infant Death Syndrome (SIDS). Through sharing her story, Gerri gives voice to the pain of child loss and the silence that often follows it. Her mission is to help bereaved parents feel seen, heard, and less alone—while also educating health professionals and the wider community on how to support grief with compassion and courage.

In addition to her writing, Gerri is the founder of Dreamlife Academy, where she supports individuals, teams, and organisations in building emotional resilience, overcoming limiting beliefs, and finding purpose after adversity. She is also a passionate advocate for raising awareness around child bereavement and continues to use her voice to create spaces for healing, learning, and growth.

A proud mother and grandmother, Gerri carries Lauren's legacy forward in everything she does—with love, honesty, and a heart wide open to life.

Acknowledgments

This book is dedicated to the memory of Lauren Claire Findell

17th January 1990 – 25th March 1990

"We shall think of Lauren often, but a future was not to be. God took her gently by the hand and whispered come with me"

A dedication by friends of Brookside March 1990, (my neighbours and friends)

I would like to express my love and gratitude to all those people who helped and supported me at the time. Especially Julie Duvnjak, the paramedics who held my hand and cried with me, Dr Jones for coming out on a mothering Sunday to pronounce Lauren's death and saving me from a heart-breaking journey to the hospital and to all my neighbours who looked after my children and me. Comforting me and supporting my grief.

To my children Carrie and Joe who have never let the memory of their sister fade and gave me a reason to keep going through difficult days. I love you both so much you mean the world to me.

Ian Moore my husband who continues to be my rock and inspiration, we met after Lauren died but I feel you know her. You are my life and the love of my life; I would be lost without you.

Finally, to my grandchildren who fill my heart with love, joy and hope. Logan, Tyrion, Amelia, Noah, Joshua, Lucas and Daisy.

This book is written with love, joy, sadness, pain and finally self-forgiveness. I truly hope it will help others understand that when the worst happens there is no need to say anything, or cross the road to avoid us, your presence and smile is the best gift you could give.

My poem.

The television was loud, and the children were laughing, I was surrounded by activity, but I felt I was all alone. Suddenly my heart sank, and I knew instinctively I knew something was wrong. My heart started pounding, the palms of my hands were clammy, and I could barely breath as I edged nearer the pram.

Perhaps I was wrong and was fearful for nothing? In a moment someone would pinch me, and I would feel silly about my gloomy thoughts. But no-one was there to break the reality.

I looked down and she was still, no movement, no smile and no cry for her milk. I was stunned, yet I was moving, hundreds of thoughts filling my head. No sense, no reason, this could not be happening.

I was a robot going through the motions, crying inside "please don't let this happen, don't let it be true." I was told I did everything, and it wasn't my fault, but I didn't believe them. It was my responsibility to make things right, to protect, to kiss and make it better. Failure was all that remained, it was true she was gone. I was screaming so loudly but the air was silent.

Gerri Moore April 1990

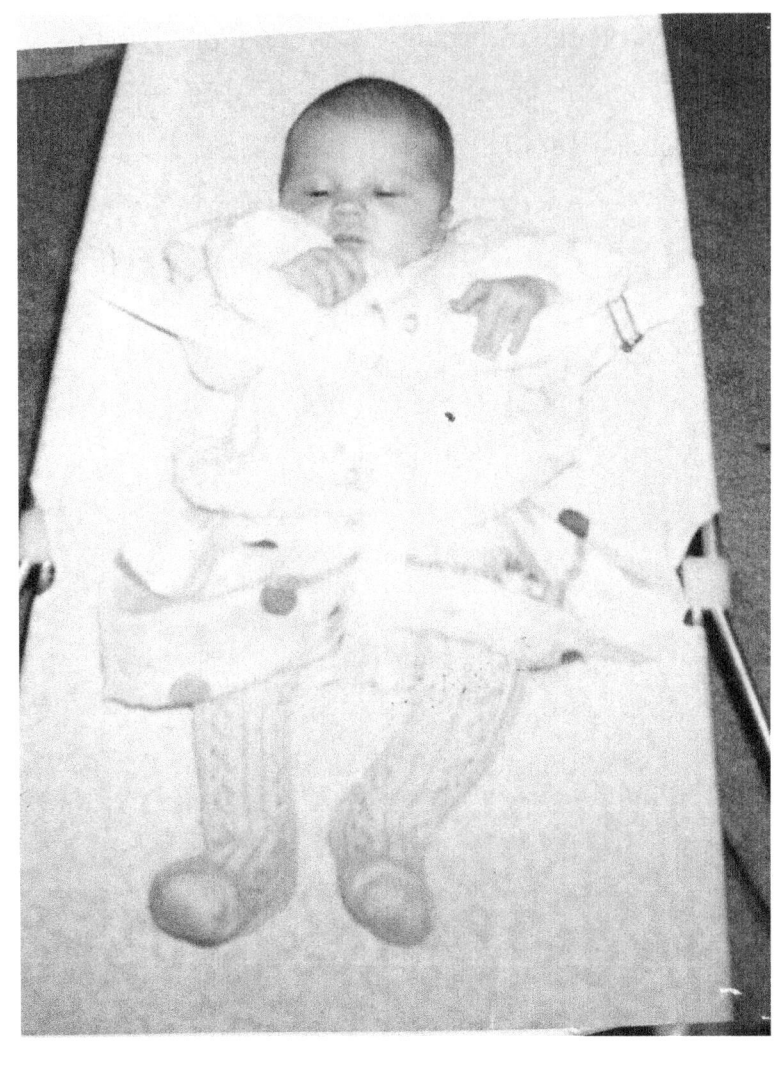

Lauren Claire Findell – Born 19/01/1990 at
Leicester Royal Infirmary

Preface

Sudden Infant Death Syndrome (SIDS) also known as "Cot Death" is the sudden and unexpected death of an apparently healthy baby. The death is unexplained, and it is estimated that around 200 babies every year die from SIDS, which makes it relatively rare. Most of the deaths occur between birth and two years, with the majority dying within the first 6 months of life.

While the cause of death is still unexplained it is believed to happen to babies who are vulnerable to certain environmental stresses. This can present with problems in how they regulate their heartbeat, breathing and temperature. It is generally reported prior to death that the child appeared well, post-mortem does not offer any concrete causes.

Support and advice are available and campaigns such as "back to sleep" have had a significant positive impact on the cases reported. The work and advice offered by the Lullaby Trust is priceless to those who have been touched by this tragedy or want to know the best way to care for their child.

The suddenness of the death results in extreme anguish, pain, feelings of failure and an overwhelming sense of loss that friends, relatives and professionals can struggle to comprehend.

This book has been written from a mother's perspective and that in no way trivialises the effects on fathers, however it is my experience and is told through my eyes. It is written in the hope that any parent who is unfortunate enough to go through this terrible ordeal will not feel alone and will feel the love and support from those of us who form a unique group of bereaved parents. It is hoped that professionals such as midwives, health visitors, emergency services and GP's will gain knowledge and skills to support parents when the worst happens.

To those who have lost a child or had to support the bereaved during this time, I offer a virtual hug and a hope that you are now in a much better place.

The Promise

The Sudden and unexpected death of a child is every parent's nightmare and a situation we do not want to think about. When this happens to you, someone you know, or you are a professional faced with having to cope with the bereaved parent. How can you understand what they are experiencing? How should you deal with the bereaved facing this nightmare?

In this book you will gain a valuable insight from the personal experience of a bereaved mother. Through the telling of her story, you will:

- Understand the emotional impact of the sudden loss of a child.
- Have a clearer understanding of the guilt a mother feels when she believes she has failed her child.
- Overcome the fear of talking to her and speaking the child's name.
- Feel the chaos she experiences when professionals and strangers enter her home, immediately after the death.

- Gain knowledge and experience from the lessons she has learnt through this tragedy.
- Change your practice to offer the best care you can at this difficult time.
- Understand there is a future for her and her family when she is given the support and care she needs. When her child's name is spoken, she will carry the child with her through her whole life.

Chapters.

1. Pregnancy & Birth

2. A lifetime in 9 weeks

3. A Mother's Day nightmare

4. Chaos & Guilt

5. After the Earthquake

6. The Funeral

7. Lessons learnt

8. Learning self-forgiveness

9. An empty Seat at the table

10. New beginnings – family, friends and

    Grandchildren

11. The Story Continues

12. A personal message to parents, health

    professionals and Lauren

Chapter 1: My pregnancy and birth.

It was May 1989 life was so busy with two small children under the age of four that I hadn't taken any notice of the signs that I may be pregnant. I was back at work part time and seemed to be endlessly rushing about with barely any time to stop and think. I was fortunate with all three pregnancies not to suffer from morning sickness, which may have been the reason I hadn't realised that I might be pregnant.

When I realised it was well over a month since my last period, I finally took time to do a pregnancy test, when it showed positive. I had a mixture of joy and fear, after all I would have to look after three children. I'm sure this is quite a common reaction as none of us know how we will cope until thrown into the deep end. I broke the news to my husband who didn't react quite as I would have expected, in fact he appeared to be quite under whelmed at the prospect of being a father again.

My due date was confirmed as 25th January 1990 which would be just three weeks after Carrie had celebrated her fourth birthday. Both children were so excited at the prospect of a new brother or sister, however their father remained uninterested and barely attended any anti-natal appointments with me.

I regularly attended my planned anti-natal checks with no major problems, just a little heart burn and occasional nausea. On the 1$^{st of}$ August 1989 I felt the baby move for the first time and from that point I was completely smitten with my tiny bundle of joy, I now started to really plan the arrival of my baby.

Everything progressed well, and I was thoroughly enjoying my pregnancy. My husband was starting to get more and more distant and barely even discussed our expected delivery. In November 1989 a routine ante-natal check showed that I had glucose in my urine. I had experienced this in previous pregnancies without concern, however this time the GP wanted to investigate further. Blood tests revealed that I had developed gestational diabetes which meant I would now have to carefully watch my diet to ensure the future development of my baby.

In December 1989 it was decided that it would be safer to deliver the baby at the Leicester Royal infirmary instead of the community hospital where I had initially been booked for delivery. The obstetricians were concerned that the baby would grow too big (a common problem when a mother has gestational diabetes) and that delivery could be problematic. I was encouraged to have my labour induced, while I wasn't keen for this to happen, I was fully aware that it was the safest option and gave my consent.

On January 3rd, 1990, Carrie celebrated her 4th birthday, it was a quiet affair with just a handful of children who came for a birthday tea. During the afternoon I started to experience contractions and was convinced that my children would share a birthday. The contractions soon stopped as they were only Braxton hicks, I must admit was glad as I wanted my children to have separate birthdays. The next week or so was calm and relaxed, as I was now on maternity leave, I didn't have to rush about, and I felt ready to deliver our third child.

On January 16th I packed my bag and went to the hospital for my planned delivery the following day. My husband barely spent any time at the hospital with me and as he had the other two children to look after left early and I didn't see him again till the next day. I don't know if you have had experienced an induction but it's not pleasant, the baby is in no rush to enter the world and yet the medics use drugs and breaking of the waters to force the delivery to happen. I must point out this is not a criticism just an observation from my experience.

Labour was slow to get going and was extremely painful, my pain threshold is not the best and so I was getting more and more distressed. The situation was not helped by the absence of my husband to share the experience and my pain. He did arrive at lunch time and so I did feel a little more comforted to have some support. Labour progressed slowly and at one point the babies heart rate started to drop giving cause for concern that an emergency caesarean would be needed. An epidural and some calming techniques with my midwife resulted in this not been necessary. Just after six o'clock in the evening I entered the second stage of labour, and my baby daughter was safely delivered at six fifteen on the 17th of January 1990.

Lauren Claire Findell was a petite baby just like her sister and brother had been and weighed in at 6lb 90z eight days early. Due to my gestational diabetes, we were kept on the delivery ward for a number of hours to monitor her blood sugars and to make sure she was feeding well. I had always struggled with breast feeding and so opted to bottle feed from the beginning. Her dad left the hospital about an hour after her birth to go and break the news to family and our other children. I was totally unaware of the shock that he would present me with only a few days later.

I was discharged from hospital three days after the birth and as her dad had forgotten the case of clothes, I had previously prepared, I was forced to take Lauren home dressed in a hospital top, a nappy and wrapped in a towel. I was totally distraught at this and later that memory would haunt me for a number of years. Carrie and Joe were so excited to look after their sister and to the outside world we had it all. This was

not the reality and the following day just four days
after her birth her dad rocked my world to its core.

Chapter 2: A lifetime in nine weeks

I was extremely tired having to get up during the night for feeds, however I was up early in the morning for the other children. I found my husband packing a bag and he calmly announced that he was leaving us and that for a number of months he had been having an affair with his sister's best friend. I remember pleading with him to stay as we wouldn't cope on our own, he would not be persuaded and left us shortly after. I just sobbed for hours and was not sure how I would cope with life

After my husband left, I was not sure how I would cope, I tried to carry on as normal but there was nothing normal about it. I felt extremely ashamed that my husband had left me and the children, and I couldn't bring myself to tell anyone that I was alone or needed help. The consequences of this were huge, I had no money, and my husband had taken any money out of the bank account that we had and therefore I couldn't afford to buy food, milk for the baby or nappies. I was definitely at my lowest point when I had to contact social services for an emergency payment to buy essentials, however I still acted as if nothing was wrong and refused to tell anyone.

It was a humiliating experience the day that the social worker arrived at my door to undertake an assessment of our needs. For the first time in my life, I had to be brutally honest that I wasn't able to cope and desperately needed a handout to pay for essentials. The social worker was a lovely lady kind and softly spoken, she held my hand and told me it would be alright and there was no shame in asking for help. I cried, I really cried knowing I was been helped for the first time in weeks.

Basic food and nappy supplies were obtained and the free milk tokens that I could use at the baby clinics were truly a life saver. I even met with Father Terry from the local catholic church and organised Lauren's Christening for Easter Sunday March 30th. So, this was it, life settled into a routine that lasted until Mother's Day March 25th when my life as I had known it changed for ever and I was never the same person again.

Chapter 3: A Mother's Day nightmare

It was Saturday 24th March 1990 and spring was definitely on its way; the children and I had experienced a typically normal day in our household. I never truly looked forward to weekends because I didn't see anyone to talk too. My neighbours were great during the week, and we often spent hours in each other company taking our kids to nursery, sharing a coffee and a chat. Weekends however were different; their partners were home, and they spent time together. yes, I was jealous as I wanted this for myself, however I did understand, but there was always a longing for Monday morning and adult company!

The 24th of March was a significant date in the diary in 1990 as it was the day that the clocks moved forward, and it heralded more day light and for me a time of new beginnings. So, as I went to bed that evening I felt for the first time since Lauren's birth a feeling that I could make it work as a single parent. The changing of the clocks meant that all three children woke later than usual on the Sunday morning, this meant I had the opportunity to spend a quite few minutes sitting in my lounge with a cup of tea and wondering what Mother's Day would be like. The tranquillity didn't last long as Lauren started crying to be fed and the other children came downstairs demanding breakfast as usual.

The next hour or so was hectic as I fed children changed Lauren and dressed her for a walk out and put her down in her pram for a sleep. My home didn't have central heating, and her pram was in the small hallway, so it was important to wrap her up for the elements in readiness for our walk. I then turned my attention to the older two children and ran us all a bath so that we could get ready. It was then that Lauren started to cry really loudly, as I couldn't leave Carrie and Joe unattended in the bathroom, I just hoped she would settle and stop crying without any intervention. After a few minutes she stopped crying, and I felt relief that I wasn't emotionally torn in making decisions about which children needed my attention. Later that day I would start to feel really guilty at not attending to Lauren, a guilt that has stayed with me ever since. I would give anything to turn back the clock and be able to go to her, cuddle her and hold her tight, not let anything happen to her and to keep her safe.

Carrie, Joe and I finished washing and got dressed and the four of us headed out to the shops for a walk. I don't think we really needed anything, but it got us out and I would be able to speak to other adults just for a few moments. This was so important when you knew that for the rest of the day it was just you and the kids. I brought the older two children some sweets and we headed home together for the remainder of mothering Sunday,

We were about halfway back when I met my neighbour who lived opposite, he was walking his dog and going to buy the Sunday papers. He asked me how I was and how the baby was doing, and I said we were all doing well, even then I didn't feel it was right to say I was on my own and life was a struggle. It is very British to keep the stiff upper lip and not put your troubles on others. To this day I wonder what the outcome would have been if he has peered inside the pram to look at the sleeping baby. Had tragedy already struck? Would the outcome have been different? Would my worst nightmare be played out on a public street in front of complete strangers? The reality was that we parted with a polite goodbye and my small family, and I continued home unaware of the life changing events that were about to unfold.

It was about 11.15am when we arrived home it was a very cold dark day, so I had left the gas fire on when we left so it would be warm for us later. I opened the double doors that led from the small hallway to the lounge and pushed the pram into the space left for it in the dining room. I left Lauren sleeping as she wasn't due a feed for about another half hour and settled the other children down to watch the TV with a drink. I took the opportunity to sit and drink a cup of coffee and have a few quite moments before feeds and lunch were due. You may wonder how I can be so detailed about events that day? Well, I have replayed every detail so many times since that every aspect in etched into my brain so hard that I will never forget it.

I remember clearly that the end of the programme the children were watching which was the "Walton's" came to an end and as the title music was playing, I looked at the clock and it was midday. Midday on Mother's Day 25th March 1990 is the moment that my life and that of my children changed for ever.

Lauren was late for her feed; this was unlike her, and she was in a steady routine and woke religiously for her milk. As I started to walk towards the pram, I suddenly got a really uneasy feeling in my stomach, there was not the small murmurings of a baby getting restless for food or the gentle movement of the pram as she wriggled. Lauren was a baby who always slept on her stomach (as the other two had) a position that was advocated at the time, so I pulled the covers back and put my hand under her stomach and lifted and turned her at the same time. I was looking straight at her face ready to smile yet was aware that her little body was very limp and as I gazed at her I noticed that she was a very strange yellow colour, and her face was flat on the side she had been lying. In that precise moment I knew she was dead and beyond saving, you see as a trained nurse I have witnessed many dead people, she had gone beyond the cyanosed state where resuscitation might help. I knew this I really did but I still hoped that somehow, I was wrong and that she would be saved, and this would all be a bad dream. At this point I let out a deafening scream for help and started to try and save my baby daughter.

I ran towards the window in the lounge and open it with such force it swung back and nearly broke, I screamed for help searching rapidly for anyone who would come to my aid. At the same time, I picked up the phone and dialled 999 begging for someone to come and help. The caller handler was really calm and was asking me lots of questions, but I remember her reassuring me that it wasn't delaying help, A neighbour of mine, a young married man with no children appeared at the window and I remember the care her took in taking Lauren from me, the kindness but fear showing in his eyes. I don't know how it made him feel being the first to help or if he still has bad thoughts about the events that day, if he reads this, I want him to know that I will be forever grateful for his help in that moment and the care and attention he gave to both Lauren and me.

All of a sudden there seemed to be several people at my door and someone urged me to let them in, at the same time I could hear the siren of the ambulance, and I was aware that Carrie and Joe had been whisked away to a neighbour's house. The paramedic arrived and took Lauren away from the caring arms of my neighbour and into the ambulance where they attempted to resuscitate her.

I don't know how long they attempted to bring her back to me, but for every second I prayed as hard as I could that she would live, and we would have a happy life together. I remember been asked where my husband was and been brutally honest that I didn't know as he had left me. I also begged someone to ring Julie who had lived next door to me for years until her recent move. Julie would know what to do as she had lost her daughter years previously.

The moment had come when I could no longer hope or dream of a different outcome, one of the paramedics came back into the room. He was a tall man in excess of six feet and as he came in, he had to stoop so as not to bang his head, he took my hand and looked me straight in the eye and told me that they could not save her despite trying everything. I don't know if I sobbed or if in that moment the enormity of events was just too much to take in, I do remember though seeing tears in that man's eyes and wanting to make it less difficult for him. I planned to ring the emergency services to express how gentle and courageous he was, but the moment was lost, and I never did. So, to whoever you were that day, thank you for helping me in a moment of despair and for trying to save my precious daughters life.

Chapter 4: Chaos and guilt.

After all the commotion for a brief moment there was an eery silence. The enormity of what had just happened wasn't sinking in. Then suddenly the noise broke through my thoughts and the noise was deafening. People were asking if I was alright, I was desperately looking for the other children to check they were okay. My GP had now arrived at the house to certify death and while he was a comforting face, I wanted him to leave so that it wouldn't be true.

I had worked in the health service for ten years as a nurse and had to deal with death and bereavement, I always believed that we hid our emotions but the realisation to me in that moment was that we weren't good at it. I looked at the faces of the professionals in my home, paramedics, doctor, police officers and every one of them had pain and anguish etched on their faces. This emotional and despairing scene was somehow comforting, I didn't feel alone, and others cared.

I wasn't prepared for the events that followed as three police officers arrived on the scene. They offered condolences but didn't explain the purpose of their visit, from my training I knew it was normal practice to attend an unexpected death, but in my shock and grief I was numb and not thinking. I remember going upstairs to use the bathroom, the door of Laurens bedroom was open, and I needed to see where she had last laid peacefully asleep. As I opened the door a police officer was in her room examining her cot, there was a sudden sharp pain in my chest. Why was he touching her precious bed and bedclothes he had no right? Then it dawned on me that he was checking that I hadn't hurt her, and her death was my fault.

The pain at this point was indescribable and suddenly tears flowed uncontrollably down my face. I remember a comforting arm placed around my shoulders and an older police officer guided me downstairs and sat me down. He held my hand in his and looked me straight in the eye, he explained that this was procedure and that they knew it was upsetting but it needed to be done. At this point he shared that he too had lost a baby to SIDS, and he looked visibly shaken and tearful, I felt an instant connection to him and knew he understood my pain without sharing words. I will forever be grateful to him that he had the courage to share a personal and painful part of his life.

When faced with the worst experience of your life you think you wouldn't be able to think, the brain is a powerful organ and almost immediately I was thinking about organ donation and how Lauren could help another child live. If I had been thinking straight, I would have known this was impossible, but I was desperate to make something good out of this awful situation. It had to be explained to me that this wasn't possible as a post-mortem would need to be performed and therefore donation was not a viable idea. The realisation that Lauren would need to be examined in this manner was like a spear being thrust through my heart, no one should touch her in this manner, she was a baby and needed gentle touches and cradling. The reality was however it is the law and therefore I had no choice.

In society the role of the mother is to care for and love her child, we have a responsibility to ensure their safety. I had failed, I had let her down and now she was dead. I kept thinking about the last 24 hours of her life, had I missed signs? Was she unwell and I should have sought medical attention? When she cried that morning if I had gone to her would she still be alive? But if I had left the other children unattended in the bath would harm have come to them? The guilt and anguish I felt was unbearable, even though others were telling me I couldn't have done anything, I didn't believe them. It felt easier to have those recriminations silently in my head. I realised years later that the feeling of pain I experienced helped me stay close to Lauren. If I hurt, then it felt she was still here and part of me.

While the police officers completed their examination of my home, I went across the road to a neighbour. They had been looking after the children, and it felt comforting to hold them in my arms and feel their warmth and heart beats. They appeared settled and were being spoilt with sweets and drinks. At this point I was constantly been asked if I knew where Lauren's dad was? As he had left me weeks previously, I had no idea. I knew that he often drank at a pub in the next village on a Sunday, so someone searched for the number and rang them.

The police contacted him and asked him to get home as soon as possible because there was a problem with one of the children. I later found out that the long drive home was filled with fear and dread as he didn't know what had happened. I don't know who told him that Lauren was dead when he did get to the house or how he reacted and to be honest at the time I didn't care. He had left me and the children; I blamed him and didn't feel he had a right to hurt. This feeling was only fleeting, he was her dad, and he needed to grieve. However, he had arrived too late to see her as the ambulance had already taken her to the hospital.

Chapter 5: After the earthquake – practicalities

Waking the next morning for a split second felt normal, in the daze of waking I forgot the events of the previous day. When realisation hit, the wave of pain was like a wrecking ball. I remember burying my head into the pillow and crying so my sobs couldn't be heard. I don't know how long it lasted but my whole body shook uncontrollably and when I finally stopped, my body hurt like it had never before and I was completely spent.

As her dad had not arrived back intime to see Lauren or hold her, we had arranged to visit the hospital to see our daughter. I was dreading this trip; I didn't want to be exposed to Stanger's and show my grief in public. However, I felt a responsibility to support her dad and reluctantly left the house to see her, one last time.

Throughout the journey and when in the hospital I cried continuously. These were not the sobs of earlier but quiet tears of pain and a deep sadness I had never experienced before. Her dad and I were shown into a waiting room next to the mortuary and we waited fearfully for what would happen next. Lauren was brought to us in a small moss's basket, covered in a white hospital blanket. Reluctantly her dad took it from the porter and laid it on the table. To this day I wish I had not made that visit and seen her again as she looked so different, and it was a memory that took me years to erase.

Lauren was still in the same clothes that I had dressed her in the previous day, her hat still hanging round her neck. This wasn't right, she was dressed in fresh clothes daily. It was her appearance that was so painful to see, her skin was waxy, and she was icy cold to the touch. It was like running your hand over marble, not what a small baby should look like and there was not that beautiful smell only a baby exudes. These feelings are personal, and I am aware that other parents feel comfort in seeing their child again. My final act was to kiss Lauren gently on her head, tell her how much I loved her, and I said goodbye.

I had always thought there was loads to do prior to a funeral and there probably is when someone has lived to an old age. We felt in limbo, waiting for the post-mortem results before we could get a death certificate and arrange the funeral. It never occurred to me that I had a choice between burial and cremation, and no one gave me advice on this. In hindsight I would have preferred to have her cremated as for years in haunted me that she lay in the cold ground when she should have been warm. I do know I wanted her laid to rest with someone and as her grandfather had died young and was buried in a double grave close by, I wanted her laid to rest with him. My mother-in-law who had remarried immediately gave her permission for us to use the plot and for this I give her my love and thanks.

The really kind police officer who himself had lost a child, was the person who visited me at home to bring the results of her post-mortem. The examination was unable to find a cause of death, Laurens's organs and body appeared normal with no signs of disease or infection. Therefore, it was officially recorded, that on the 25th of March 1990 the cause of death was sudden infant death syndrome.

On the afternoon of the 28^{th of} March, I attended a beautifully peaceful registry office in Market Bosworth to formally register the death of my daughter. These official acts that feel very scary and dauting at the time, brought me an immense comfort over the years that I did everything for her from birth till her death. Never having arranged a funeral before I did not know where to begin. If you are ever faced with doing this or advising others, then pick a good undertaker and they will guide you through the whole process.

We chose a small family run undertakers in our village and they were amazing. They communicated with me constantly, told me when they were collecting Lauren from the hospital and that she was laying peacefully in their chapel of rest. I did enquire about seeing her prior to the funeral and was advised against it. This really gentle man said that the scaring from the post-mortem meant she wouldn't look the same and I might get distressed. I valued his honesty at the time and have never regretted my decision.

I wanted Lauren to look beautiful to be finally laid to rest and chose her christening gown which she never got to wear as she died before this could happen. The day I attended the registry office I had gone into a beautiful small children's store and brought her a pair of paints with butterflies on them. I wanted to give her wings to make the flight to heaven easier. The assistant asked if they were for my baby and that she would look lovely in them. I couldn't upset her by saying they were to bury my baby in, but I'm convinced she saw the tears in my eyes. Even today if I see a butterfly, I think Lauren is letting me know she is okay.

If you have dealt with the death of a loved one, I am sure that the support you gain from a friend, priest or officiant has been important. I was extremely lucky to have the local catholic priest as support. He offered comfort and support, especially regarding her not been christened. He allowed me to pick the music and readings and for us to bury her with small notes from family and gifts from her brother and sister. The comfort this gave me then and now cannot be expressed in words. I would like to express my love and thanks for his kindness and support.

Chapter 6: The Funeral

The day of the funeral arrived, and I wasn't sure how I was going to get through it. There seemed to be chaos in the house, so much noise and movement, I felt I needed to escape for a few moments to re centre myself and my emotions. I decided to walk to the local shop and buy a bottle of whiskey for guests after the funeral, as I paid the shop keeper looked and said, "smile it might never happen." I remember those words so clearly and thinking but it already has, but I said nothing as the excruciating pain I was experiencing was to raw and real to share with a stranger.

We drove the few short miles to the catholic church, it was so peaceful and there was a beauty about the simplicity of the Church with light streaming through the window, but inside I felt like my heart was ripping apart and I had an overwhelming urge to run away and not be part of this painful experience. Of course, I didn't run, how could I Lauren deserved my final act of love.

I had chosen not to take her brother and sister too the funeral as I didn't feel that I could cope with managing my own grief and be able to look after them too. Carrie has since told me that she felt I made the wrong decision, and she should have been there. I apologise to her if that has hurt her, but I did what I thought was best at the time and I think self-preservation was all I was capable of at the time.

We were supported at the funeral by some really special friends, neighbours and family, but as her dad and I waited at the entrance doors for her to arrive we couldn't have felt more lonely or isolated in our pain and grief. As the funeral car arrived her dad walked out and took the tiny white coffin in his arms and for the final time he carried our daughter into the church.

I find it difficult to explain the inner turmoil that I felt at witnessing this tiny white satin covered box being carried and knowing that a once beautiful and vibrant baby girl now lay in it as her final resting place, my whole body ached, and I felt I would never feel at peace again.

The service was simple and beautiful, there were no speeches or eulogies, just beautiful music, prayers, and the poem footsteps in the sand written by Mary Stevenson.

One night I dreamed
I was walking along the beach with the Lord.
Many scenes from my life flashed across the sky.
In each case I noticed footprints in the sand.
Sometimes there were two sets of footprints,
Other times there were one set of footprints.

This bothered me because I noticed
That during the low periods of my life,
When I was suffering from anguish, sorrow, or defeat,
I could only see one set of prints.

So, I said to the lord,
"You promised me lord that if I followed you,
You would walk with me always.
But I noticed that during the trying periods of my life,
There have only been one set of footprints in the
sand.

Why when I needed you most have you not been
there for me?"
The Lord replied.
"The times when you have seen only one set of
Footprints in the sand,
Is when I carried you."

I found this such a comforting poem at the time and whether or not you are religious, if you are going through a difficult time, I hope you know there are friends, family or people who care that want to carry you through those difficult moments.

As a family we were supported that day by members of the church congregation, people I didn't know who came out to show us love and care. These same people over many months would pick me up to go to church on a Sunday so we weren't alone and make tea and play with my children and showed such compassion and love. I was honoured and grateful that they supported me when I needed it most.

The drive from the church to the cemetery seemed so long and very quiet, we knew that this was the final act of what had been such a painful and dreadful time. Standing by the open grave I felt like my life had ended and I would never feel happy or smile again. Watching the tiny white coffin being lowered into the ground was a living nightmare, I did find comfort in knowing she was laid to rest with her grandfather and the single red rose that was laid on her coffin signified a lifetime of giving Lauren love that was taken away from me.

Later when we gathered with friends and family at my home, I felt a sense of relief that I had managed to get through the funeral and that I was now at home with her brother and sister. I held them much tighter that night and that gave me some comfort on the most challenging of days. Lauren's name was spoken often that day and I am grateful for every person who spoke of her and shared their love with me.

Chapter 7: Lessons learnt.

It is now many years since Lauren was so suddenly and cruelly wrenched away from me and I no longer have the intense and unrelenting pain that I experienced back then. I remember someone telling me at the time that you never get over the death of your child, but you do learn to live your life without them. My experience has been that I gradually stopped hurting constantly, and I eventually was able to smile and laugh again. This took a long time to happen, and I was changed forever by her dying, but the pain reduced over time and now I can think of her and smile.

I chose to say her name often and others have spoken her name to me. A very wise counsellor once told me that by taking the person through your life with you and not pretending it didn't happen will help you with your grief, and I was very thankful for that advice.

Death remains a taboo subject, and I have found that people don't want to contemplate the loss of a child and think if they don't talk about it then it won't happen. But the reality is that is does happen and I have found that when I talk about losing a child that I have discovered that it has happened to that person or someone they know. The relief that someone else feels when they have permission to talk about their child and the love, they feel for them is palpable, so please don't be afraid to say the child's name, ask someone how they are on their child's birthday. It won't hurt us or make us feel any sadder than we already do, but we will thank you for remembering and caring enough to say something.

When a child dies, there is a personal and collective grief. It shakes our sense of what's natural. It turns the world upside down. We expect to outlive our parents, not our children and when that order is disrupted, it creates a grief that's almost impossible to describe. It's not just the loss of a life, it's the loss of dreams, of milestones, of a future imagined but never lived.

In society, we often struggle to talk about death—especially the death of a baby or infant. It can feel like a taboo subject, and because of that, parents can feel unseen, unheard, and isolated in their grief. The baby may not have been known widely, but to the parents, that child was already everything. Their presence mattered, and so does their absence.

There's an intimacy to that kind of loss, the smell of the baby's skin, the touch of tiny fingers, the sound of their cry. Letting go of those sensory connections can be overwhelming. The practicalities of dismantling the nursery, giving away clothes, unused nappies, bottles, and milk, can feel like another kind of grief altogether. Every object holds meaning. Every decision feels final.

Some parents find it comforting to maintain a continuing bond with their child, to carry them through life in conversation, rituals, photos, and memory. Saying their name, telling others about them, including them when asked how many children you have, it can be cathartic. It's a way to honour them. To keep them part of your world.

But not everyone understands. And that can make conversations awkward or painful. So, we sometimes go into survival mode, coping in bite-size pieces, just getting through the day, faking it until we can function again. It's not weakness; it's human.

Then there are the difficult questions: Do we try for another child? What if it happens again? What about our other children, how do we protect them, and ourselves, from more pain? I do not have the answers to such a profound question; however, I have heard people say that the price of loving someone is the pain of grief. I resonate with this and am grateful for the moments the pain resurfaces briefly, as it is a reminder that I loved her.

As I mentioned at the beginning this is written from a mother's perspective, however it's important to say fathers grieve too. Their voices and their pain matter. They may express it differently, but they feel it deeply. Too often their needs are overlooked in the focus on the mother.

Campaigns like Back to Sleep remind us that this tragedy has happened to others, and we are not alone. But even with that knowledge, each loss is personal. It's ours. It leaves a scar, not visible to others but we are aware of it daily.

For some, events like the 1991 organ retention scandal, re-opened wounds long thought closed. I remember receiving a letter from the hospital inviting me to attend a meeting. It was at the Leicester City Football ground, and I sat in a room overlooking the pitch and was told that tissue from her organs had been retained. At that moment I recall a searing pain in my chest that took me back to the day she died. The message is that grief doesn't move in a straight line. It re-emerges when we least expect it.

That's why the little things matter so much, like hearing our child's name used by professionals or being gently asked about our experience. Don't be afraid to ask. We don't want to forget, we want to remember. We want you to understand. Because this has already happened to us, and if there's something to be learned from our story, please learn it.

We want to talk.

We want to be seen.

We want to be heard.

We want to feel, because that pain is all we have left of them.

And in feeling it, we keep them close.

Chapter 8: Learning self-forgiveness

When your child dies suddenly and without warning, especially through something like sudden infant death syndrome (SIDS), you're plunged into a world of unknowns. You're desperate for answers, for something to hold onto. I remember sitting with the paediatrician after the postmortem, needing clarity, longing for logic in a situation where there was none. Despite kind words, facts and details from the postmortem I still didn't have the answers I craved and ached for.

They explained what they could. That it wasn't my fault. That it happens quickly, quietly, without suffering. That Lauren had shown no signs of an illness I may have been unaware of. But nothing could quite soothe the ache of "why her?" It took time to believe them, (many years actually) to really believe I didn't miss something, that I hadn't failed her.

People often talk about how strong I was, I know at the time I didn't feel strong, I felt lost, confused and so very lonely. Later I did realise the strength I did possess, but it was not a loud strength. It's not bold or brave or defiant. It's quiet. It's waking up the next morning. It's taking a breath. It's sitting with the pain and letting it wash over me without drowning. It's looking after my other children and holding the tears and the screams until they are safely tucked up in bed asleep. It's stifling the sobs and the screams, so no one hears, without my husband there was no one to hold me or tell me it was fine to let go, which was an added burden. That kind of resilience doesn't come from wanting to be strong. It comes from love and the need to survive and move forward.

I moved forward, inch by inch. Some days, simply getting out of bed felt like a triumph. Other days I could enjoy the presence of others and the joy of living. I remember feeling like I was crumbling and falling apart when I saw babies with their parents, asking why are they here and Lauren isn't? With time this changed and I found myself feeling an inner warmth and a stirring of joy that those parents did not experience the loss of a child as I had.

I celebrate Lauren's birthday every year. I honour the moments we had. I say her name, light candles, and talk about her with love. Not as a tragedy, but as a little girl who was here, who changed my world in her short time on earth. She's not defined by her death— she's remembered for her life. That's important to me. It's how I keep her present, how I bring her with me into my future.

Grief isn't linear. It revisited me. Sometimes unexpectedly. A smell, a story, a date on the calendar. I remember watching the Emmerdale storyline with Laurel and Ashley losing a baby to SIDS and feeling it all come rushing back. As I watched the actors play out the scenes it was like watching the events of Laurens death play out right in front of me. The rawness. The ache. The confusion. But also, the recognition. Seeing grief reflected back to me reminded me I'm not alone. That my story matters. It should matter to every health professional and to parents who are unfortunate enough to live through the unexpected death of their child.

Grief doesn't leave; it softens. It comes in waves, but eventually, I learnt to float. I found joy again in the simple things and I smiled, but don't be fooled because the pain and dismay can rear its head without warning. However, as time passes it will be momentary and at times it will stay a little longer. I am thankful for it as it reminds me, I care, I love, and I haven't forgotten Lauren.

When I met Ian, it was many years after Lauren's passing, and he had never had the opportunity to know her or to love her. He was never afraid to ask me about her or to understand my grief and my pain and to come to terms with a loss of a child that he would have known as father. I only have a few small precious photos and a video of her that lasts a minute or so, taken in the first few weeks of her life, we have shared this, and it has given him an insight into the beautiful daughter who was taken too soon. I need to be really clear that he has also grieved for a child he never knew. Ian and I had to learn how to grieve together, even though we grieved differently. I had guilt I couldn't speak out loud. He carried pain I couldn't see.

We talked. We cried. We held silence together. That emotional sharing didn't come easy, but it was real. We didn't have all the answers, but we gave each other permission to feel without judgement.

Grieving isn't about forgetting. It's about understanding. Accepting. Living alongside the loss. It's learning to speak about her with love and without shame. To tell people, "Yes, I had a daughter," and not feel the need to hide or explain. It's re-mapping who I am, not just as a mother, but as a bereaved parent. That identity carries weight for me but also honour. It's part of my truth and who I am.

There was a time when I wondered if talking about her made people uncomfortable. I worried about being "that person" the one who brings sadness into the room. But I've learned not to carry shame for loving my daughter loudly and unapologetically. I cannot know how someone else will react and I have found that I no longer hold responsibility for them. This may appear cruel, it's not meant to be as I do care about them, but by not speaking up I am denying the existence of my child.

I speak about her in positive terms. Her life was short, but it was beautiful. She brought light into my world. That light doesn't vanish just because she's gone, it is more like it is hidden behind a curtain and when I feel brave enough I pull it back and let it flood in.

Perhaps the hardest truth to accept is that I did everything I could. I loved her. I cared for her. I watched over her. And it still happened. That was never in my control. There's freedom in that acceptance—not because it makes the loss easier, but because it lifts the weight of guilt that never belonged to me.

The training I have completed in recent years in NLP (Neuro Linguistic Programming) and particularly in timeline resourcing where I have learnt to let go of negative emotions that do not serve me, has further cemented this freedom of acceptance. Thank you to Mark and Nicky Taylor of the Taylored Life Company for opening my world to this amazing experience, that has given me peace and a new perspective on past events.

My Final Thoughts.

Her life mattered. My grief is part of my love story with her.
And though the world may move on, I carry her always, through every milestone, every conversation, every quiet moment of remembrance.

I am not just a mother who lost a child.
I am a mother who still loves a child.
And that love? That never ends.

Chapter 9: An empty seat at the table

Family Celebrations: The Empty Chair. There is always someone missing.

At birthdays, Christmases, anniversaries, there's a quiet echo in the room where she should be. And though others might not notice it, I do. I always do.

Family photos are beautiful, yes, but they're never whole. I've learned to smile in them, to be present in those joyful moments, but there's always that ache deep inside me. One less face. One less laugh. One less story added to the family album.

What's hardest is not the memories we had, but the ones we never got to make. There's no sense of her future. No first day at school, no first love, no exams, no ambitions to nurture. And yet, I find myself picturing her and dreaming about the person she would become.

I look at her siblings and wonder, would she have had that same smile? That quiet determination? The stubbornness or wanting to push boundaries.

I imagine how she might have looked like as a teenager, what her voice would have sounded like now. These imagined milestones hurt—but they also connect me to her. They keep her close.

For me Mother's Day is a Day of Love, and Loss, at the same time it is joyous for the children I still have in my life.

Mother's Day haunts me. It never falls on the same date, but my grief is constant every year. While others are opening cards and being treated to breakfast in bed, there's a part of my heart that feels heavy. Because one of my children isn't here to say, "I love you, Mum."

Even now, I walk past the card aisle and feel the urge to buy something from her, for her. That ache doesn't go. The desire to mother doesn't end, it lives alongside me.

As a family we have passed many milestones she never reached, but I have silently celebrated anyway. When she would've turned 18, I lit a candle. I said her name. I imagined what she might have worn. I let myself grieve and celebrate all at once. When she would've been 21, I did the same. Because those milestones still matter. She still matters. I've known when she would have received her exam results. I've marked them quietly. The world didn't know, but I did. I always will.

I carry her with me every day, through my work, my relationships, my growth. She shaped me in ways no one sees. I turn around when I hear her name, as if she might walk in the room. I feel her when I'm quiet and still. She travels through life with me. Not in body, but in spirit. Always.

When people ask how many children I have, I include her. Every time.
And if someone says something that dismisses her existence, I gently but firmly correct them. Because she lived. Because she was real. Because pretending otherwise would be to deny her, and I won't do that.

This wasn't *God's will*. It wasn't fate, or a lesson, or a blessing in disguise (as many people said, when they were trying to be kind) . It was a loss. A deep, painful, life-altering loss. And I honour her not by pretending it was meant to be, but by telling the truth, the raw and painful truth.

She lived. She mattered. She is loved.

Chapter 10: New Beginnings – family and Grandchildren

A New Chapter in my life. But Never Without Her

Life didn't stop. It shifted. I have had new relationships, new roles, new learning, each a part of my life which is still unfolding. And yet, in every new beginning, she is there with me. Quietly present. Her influence woven into every decision, every change, every step forward. My worry about my children experiencing the same loss, when my first grandchild Logan stayed with us, listening to his breathing and fearing that it would stop.

It was all fine, however my lived experience had made me realise that no matter who you are disaster can strike, and it is prudent to take all the measures you can to avoid it. That is why I still follow the Lullaby Trust and try and share this knowledge with others.

Going back to study, stepping into new jobs, building new dreams, these were not acts of moving on. They were acts of honouring her. Choosing to live well, because she could not. They were about living for those who still remained and who deserved to be seen.

There is something special about watching my other children grow. Every milestone they reach carries its own weight, challenges, pain, joy, pride, gratitude and an ever-present thought of what might have been if Lauren had lived.

But it makes me pay attention more closely. I see them, really see them. I cherish every emotion, every challenge, every triumph. Their lives remind me daily that love can hold both happiness and heartache at the same time. And that is a truth I've come to live by. I may not have always got it right or made the decisions that I could have made with hindsight, but I can put my hand on my heart and say I did the best I could with the skills and knowledge I had at the time.

I've learned to seek peace and forgiveness in the quiet moments. Blue skies. Warm sunshine on my skin. The sound of birds singing as a new day begins. These moments are whispers from Lauren. Reminders that life still holds beauty, and that I am allowed to feel it. When a butterfly is nearby, I know she is sending me love.

Sometimes I just sit, letting the breeze carry my thoughts, giving space to remember her, to speak with her in silence. That private time is precious. It's where I reconnect with myself. With her. With the life we shared, however briefly.

I no longer just mourn my daughter, I celebrate her. I speak about her proudly. I remember her milestones. I share her story not from a place of pain alone, but from a place of deep love. Her life, as short as it was, changed me. Gave me new purpose. Brought clarity. Lit a fire within me to make a difference. It did however leave me with void that cannot be filled by anyone else, an ache that cannot be taken away with pain killers, a sorrow that at times I carry silently. Yet I carry these with pride, because without having carried

Lauren for nine months and caring for her for 9 weeks they would not exist and neither would she. They are the reminder of her life and the joy she gave me, so do not attempt to take them away or try and get me to forget as I will not let you.

This grief carved out a new direction. And I followed it, sometimes blindly but always with courage, with compassion, and with commitment to becoming more of who I truly am. There came a time when I stopped apologising for my story. I embraced who I was before her, and who I've become since. A woman who has endured. A mother who has loved fiercely. A human who continues to rise, again and again. Yes, I fall but I am able to pick myself up and try again, this is because of all of you who have loved me, supported me and spoken Lauren's name with me.

There is no shame in sorrow. And no weakness in vulnerability. I stand stronger now because I allowed myself to feel it all. If you are currently experiencing the raw grief of a similar loss, I feel your pain and wish you peace and tranquillity in the future.

The birth of grandchildren brought a fresh wave of emotion for me, a new kind of love, and a tenderness that only deepens with time. I remember feeling fearful of history repeating but was able to embrace this new life and the joy that it gave me. Watching this new generation grow, I feel such heartfelt joy and pride. They remind me that love multiplies. That the human spirit can conquer, even when confronted by the worst of events.

Life has been a rollercoaster. Not just because of her loss, but because of all the other challenges that followed, more bereavements, hard decisions, the moments where I didn't have the answers. I won't pretend it's always been graceful or easy, it hasn't. But I have been able to feel love, hope and optimism after such a life changing event, I put this down to the love and support I have received from many different people in my life.

I have kept showing up. For my family. For myself. For my purpose. I strive to grow. To learn. To live with intention. And to use what I've experienced not as a burden—but as a catalyst to help others, through my coaching work and my NLP practice.

Chapter 11: The story continues

There is no perfect ending to my story, because love doesn't end, and neither does grief. What there is, however, is a continuing.

A continuing of life.
A continuing of love.
A continuing of Lauren's legacy—through me, through those I love, and through the work I now feel signifies who I am now. Also now through this book and my sharing personal, emotional and truthful parts of my life, some which have never previously been shared openly.

I have been through pain I never imagined. I have known the stillness of a nursery never needed; the silence of a name unspoken. I have felt the ache of time moving forward without the one who should have been part of every milestone.

But I have also known joy. Deep, grounding, beautiful joy.

The kind that comes from watching my children become who they were meant to be.
The kind that arrives with laughter in unexpected places, in soft summer evenings, in arms wrapped around grandchildren. Their laughter and their success.
The kind of joy that doesn't erase sorrow but lives alongside it.

My story is one of heartbreak and healing. Of love found, lost, and reimagined. Of grief that shaped me and gave me direction. Of a little girl whose presence was brief, but whose impact was eternal.

Her life was a spark.
And from that spark, a fire was lit in me—a fire to live fully, to love deeply, to speak truth, and to help others find their voice in the world.

I have built a life around that. Not in spite of the pain, but because of it.

Grief has changed its shape over the years. From rawness to reflection. From sorrow to story. It's still there, but softer, steadier, now walking side by side with gratitude and acceptance of my life's events as they unfolded.

Through new relationships, career paths, friendships, and the next generation being born, I have come to see the beauty of the life and the despair of grief. Joy and sorrow. Light and dark. Endings and new beginnings.

I've had to learn to let go of what could have been and embrace the life I have lived, but I've gained something too. A deep understanding of what matters. A profound appreciation for simple moments. The courage to keep going, even when the path is unclear or difficult. I have learned to stand up for myself and not to be afraid of using my voice. My model of the world has been shaped and influenced by the events of Laurens life and sudden death. I am who I am because of them.

There are still new joys to come. New adventures. New milestones. New memories to make with those I hold dear. And I will carry Lauren with me, always. I no longer ask, "why me?" I simply say, "This is part of my story. And I choose to honour it." I will continue on this journey—with strength, with compassion, and with a heart wide open to love, in all its forms. I will keep telling her story. I will keep living mine.

And I will keep walking forward, with grace, with gratitude, and with hope.

Because that's what she would want.
Because that's what I have become.
And because life, despite it all, is still beautiful and I cherish it.

I have written my story and laid bare my emotions, not for sympathy but to shine a light on the truth of losing a child and their future. So that one mother or father can read this and feel less alone and isolated. So that health professionals can support grieving parents with a little less fear, with the confidence that the small gestures and words will be remembered and held close for all the years to come.

This is my story; my truth and it is told from the heart. Writing it has been both painful, emotional, cathartic and energising, as I remember those that have supported me and guided me in the years since Laurens death.

Lauren, Claire Findell, you are loved, you are missed, and you are cherished. I hold you close to my heart and in every breath I take. I love you Mum

Chapter 12: A personal message to parents, professionals and to Lauren.

Dear Parent,

There are no words that can truly ease the pain of losing your child but please know this: you are not alone.

What you're feeling right now is raw, overwhelming, and utterly life changing. And that's okay. There is no guidebook, no right or wrong way to grieve. Some days you might feel numb, other days completely broken, and occasionally, you may smile and feel guilty for doing so. That, too, is okay.

You may find comfort in silence. Or in speaking your child's name a hundred times a day. You might want to pack away their things gently or keep everything exactly as it was. Whatever you choose it's valid. Your way is the right way for you.

There is no timeline. No finish line. Grief changes shape, but it never truly disappears. Yet over time, you may find little sparks of light again. Joy in simple moments, a sense of your child's presence in unexpected ways, and strength you never imagined you had.

You are still a parent. That love didn't end—it just looks different now.

Be gentle with yourself. Allow the bad days, and don't question the good ones. You're not failing. You're surviving. And I promise, others walk beside you, even if you can't see them yet.

With all my heart,
Gerri Moore

Dear Health Professional,

I want to thank you, for showing up in one of the most difficult spaces imaginable.

Supporting a parent whose child has died is not easy. You may worry about saying the wrong thing, or fear that showing emotion is unprofessional. But I want to reassure you: your presence and your humanity are far more important than getting the words exactly right.

Please, say the child's name. Don't shy away from it. To that parent, their child is still very real. Saying their name brings them back into the room, even for a moment. It says, your child mattered.

Don't be afraid of your tears. Your compassion is a gift. Parents remember kindness. They remember when someone looked them in the eye and didn't flinch. They remember when they were treated as more than just patients, but as grieving parents, navigating an unbearable moment.

And as you care for others, please remember to care for yourself.

You are human. What you witness stays with you. Take the time to reflect, to debrief, to process your own feelings. You're not expected to carry it all alone. Reach out. Be supported, too.

You make more of a difference than you may ever realise. And for that, I thank you deeply.

With respect and compassion,
Gerri Moore

A Personal Message to Lauren

From Mum

My darling Lauren,

Not a day passes when I don't think of you. Though your time here was heartbreakingly short, your presence changed me in ways I could never have imagined. From the moment I felt you move inside me, I knew you were special your tiny heartbeat was the rhythm that softened the chaos around me and reminded me that love could be quiet, gentle, and powerful all at once.

Losing you shattered my world. The silence where your cry should have been, the stillness where your breath once rose and fell—it left an ache so deep, I feared I might never find my way back. But through the darkness, I found that your light still flickered gently within me. And even now, decades later, I feel you with me.

In the flutter of a butterfly, I see your spirit. In the warmth of the sun on my face, I feel your love. In the laughter of your brother and sister, in the tiny hands of your nieces and nephews you are everywhere. You have walked beside me through every moment of healing, through every triumph and setback, in every conversation where I've shared your name with pride.

Your presence has shaped me as a mother, a woman, and a coach. It's because of you that I understand the depth of loss and the miracle of hope. You've given me the courage to speak the unspeakable and the strength to carry others through their own grief. You've shown me that love doesn't end it transforms. And so, I carry you. Always.

Your name is woven into my story, your memory etched into every beat of my heart. You are my daughter. You are my light. And though this world didn't get the chance to know you, I will make sure it never forgets you.

I love you with every part of me. I miss you in every quiet moment.
And I feel you, my beautiful girl, in everything that still lives on.

With all my love,
Mum

Thank you.

I would like to thank all my family and friends who continue to be my rock, my inspiration and my shoulder to cry on when needed.

Thank you to all the health professionals who looked after me during my pregnancy, the loss of Lauren and those who continue to support me through life.

To my children, I love you even when you think otherwise, I might not always agree with your actions, but I will always love you.

The biggest thanks go to the professionals, parents and the bereaved who have taken the time to read my story. I hope it has given you what you need to cope during the darkest period someone is going through.

To the bereaved mothers who read this, I am thinking of you, and I feel your pain. You are not alone, I wish you well as you navigate your life following the death of your child. Look after yourselves and those you love.

Love Gerri.

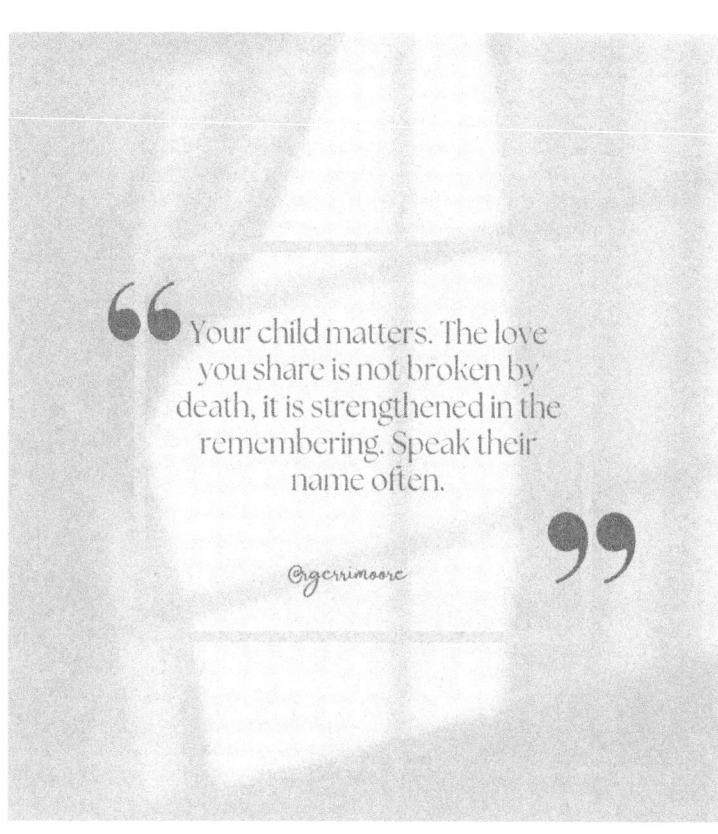

"Your child matters. The love you share is not broken by death, it is strengthened in the remembering. Speak their name often.

@gerrimoore

Printed in Great Britain
by Amazon

63359151R00047